The Essential Einstein

Edited by

J. MANHIRE

ISBN: 1494724405
ISBN-13: 978-1494724405

For Ann.

CONTENTS

PREFACE

The following is a collection of quotations attributed to Albert Einstein. They are the "essentials" in as much as they illuminate Einstein the man...or at least Einstein the icon...since by his own admission, many of the quotes attributed to him are things he wished he had said, but never did. Most of us are aware of Einstein's contributions to physics, even if we do not fully understand them. But the reason you are reading this book is to know more about Einstein the philosopher, thinker, activist, and at times, humorist, as well as Einstein the scientist.

To that end I tried to compile quotations by topics that I believe best reflect the core principles of Einstein the man: happiness, love, science, imagination, humanity, education, war, politics, and religion. In addition, I have added some of Einstein's thoughts on aging, a topic on which he became very reflective in the last decade or so of his life.

Since Einstein's icon is as visual as it is ideological, I have peppered the text with images. Some may be known to you, while others may be new. I have also endeavored to attribute the quotes that I could to citable sources to maximize the authenticity of each quote for you. There are many versions of Einstein's quotes floating around, and I tried the best I could to deliver for you the "true" quote.

So let's begin. Even if you consume the entire contents in one sitting, I encourage you to use this small book as a companion that you carry and refer back to often. As with the sayings of many great spirits, you will most certainly get something new out of Einstein's wisdom each time you read it.

J. Manhire
Stafford, Virginia
December 2013

1

ON A HAPPY LIFE

A happy man is too satisfied with the present to dwell too much on the future.[1]

If there is no price to be paid, it is also not of value.[2]

Arrows of hate have been aimed at me too, but they have never hit me, because somehow they belonged to another world with which I have no connection whatsoever.[3]

Try to become not a man of success, but try rather to become a man of value.[4]

If you want to live a happy life, tie it to a goal, not to people or objects.[5]

-----

[1] From "My Future Plans," September 18, 1896. *The Collected Papers of Albert Einstein*, Vol. 1, Doc. 22.

[2] Aphorism, June 27, 1920. *Albert Einstein Archives* 36–582.

[3] Quoted in *Portraits & Self-Portraits*, by George Schreiber 1935–1936. *Albert Einstein Archives* 28–332.

[4] Quoted by William Miller in *Life Magazine*, May 2, 1955.

[5] Quoted by Ernst Straus in French, *Einstein: A Centenary Volume*, 32.

A life directed chiefly toward the fulfillment of personal desires will sooner or later always lead to bitter disappointment.[6]

---

[6] To T. Lee, January 16, 1954. *Albert Einstein Archives* 60–235.

―――

Whoever is careless with truth in small matters can not be trusted in important affairs.[7]

―――

Personally, I experience the greatest degree of pleasure in having contact with works of art. They furnish me with happy feelings of an intensity that I cannot derive from other sources.

―――

He who has never been deceived by a lie does not know the meaning of bliss.[8]

―――

I am very happy with my new home in friendly America and in the liberal atmosphere of Princeton.[9]

―――

The trite objects of human efforts—possessions, superficial success, luxury—have always seemed contemptible to me.[10]

―――

I was originally supposed to become an engineer, but the thought of having to expend my creative energy on things that make practical everyday life even more refined, with a loathsome capital gain as the goal, was unbearable to me.[11]

―――

---

[7] From draft of address on the occasion of the 7th anniversary of Israel's independence, April 1955. *Albert Einstein Archive* 60–003.

[8] To Elsa Löwenthal, April 30, 1912, *Collected Papers of Albert Einstein*, Vol. 5, Doc. 389.

[9] Quoted in "Survey Graphic," 24 (August 1935) 384, 413.

[10] From "The World As I See It," (1930), reprinted in *Ideas and Opinions*, 9.

[11] To Heinrich Zangger, 1918. *Collected Papers of Albert Einstein*, Vol. 8, Doc. 597.

THE ESSENTIAL EINSTEIN

2

ON SCIENCE & KNOWLEDGE

All of science is nothing more than refinement of everyday thinking.[1]

———

The creative principle [of science] resides in mathematics.[2]

———

I became more and more convinced that even nature could be understood as a relatively simple mathematical structure.[3]

———

The content of scientific theory itself offers no moral foundation for the personal conduct of life.[4]

———

The more one chases the quanta, the better they hide themselves.[5]

———

All my life I have dealt with objective matters; hence I lack both the natural aptitude and the experience to deal properly with people and to carry out official functions.[6]

---

[1] From "Physics and Reality," 1936.

[2] From "On the Method of Theoretical Physics" (1933), reprinted in *Ideas and Opinions*, 274.

[3] Quoted in *The Tower*, April 13, 1935.

[4] From "Science and God: A Dialogue," in *Forum and Century* 83 (1930), 373.

[5] To Paul Ehrenfest, July 12, 1924. *Albert Einstein Archives* 10–089.

[6] To Abba Eban, November 18, 1952. *Albert Einstein Archives* 28–943.

––––

The grand aim of all science is to cover the greatest number of empirical facts by logical deduction from the smallest number of hypotheses or axioms.[7]

––––

If we knew what it was we were doing, it would not be called research, would it?

––––

The most beautiful experience we can have is the mysterious – the fundamental emotion which stands at the cradle of true art and true science.

––––

Everything must be made as simple as possible, but not simpler.

––––

It would be possible to describe everything scientifically, but it would make no sense; it would be without meaning, as if you described a Beethoven symphony as a variation of wave pressure.

––––

One thing I have learned in a long life: that all our science, measured against reality, is primitive and childlike – and yet it is the most precious thing we have.

––––

Energy cannot be created or destroyed, it can only be changed from one form to another.

––––

Information is not knowledge.

––––

As far as the laws of mathematics refer to reality, they are not certain; and as far as they are certain, they do not refer to reality.

––––

A little knowledge is a dangerous thing. So is a lot.

–––––––––––

[7] Quoted in *Life Magazine*, January 9, 1950.

———

No amount of experimentation can ever prove me right; a single experiment can prove me wrong.

———

Pure mathematics is in its way the poetry of logical ideas.

———

Technological progress is like an axe in the hands of a pathological criminal.

———

You do not really understand something unless you can explain it to your grandmother.

———

Creating a new theory is not like destroying an old barn and erecting a skyscraper in its place. It is rather like climbing a mountain, gaining new and wider views, discovering unexpected connections between our starting points and its rich environment. But the point from which we started out still exists and can be seen, although it appears smaller and forms a tiny part of our broad view gained by the mastery of the obstacles on our adventurous way up.

———

If at first the idea is not absurd, then there is no hope for it.

———

We are in the position of a little child entering a huge library, whose walls are covered to the ceiling with books in many different languages. The child knows that someone must have written those books. It does not know who or how. It does not understand the the languages in which they are written. The child notes a definite plan in the arrangement of the books, a mysterious order, which it does not comprehend but only dimly suspects.

———

The only source of knowledge is experience.

———

Setting an example is not the main means of influencing others, it is the only means.

―――

If I had an hour to solve a problem I'd spend 55 minutes thinking about the problem and 5 minutes thinking about solutions.

―――

The most beautiful thing we can experience is the mysterious. It is the source of all true art and science. He to whom the emotion is a stranger, who can no longer pause to wonder and stand wrapped in awe, is as good as dead — his eyes are closed. The insight into the mystery of life, coupled though it be with fear, has also given rise to religion. To know what is impenetrable to us really exists, manifesting itself as the highest wisdom and the most radiant beauty, which our dull faculties can comprehend only in their most primitive forms — this knowledge, this feeling is at the center of true religiousness.

―――

Those who have the privilege to know have the duty to act.

―――

When the number of factors coming into play in a phenomenological complex is too large, scientific method in most cases fails. One need only think of the weather, in which case the prediction even for a few days ahead is impossible.

―――

3

ON CURIOSITY & IMAGINATION

The important thing is to not stop questioning. Curiosity has its own reason for existing.[1]

———

Violence sometimes may have cleared away obstructions quickly, but it never has proved itself creative.[2]

———

Logic will get you from A to Z; imagination will get you everywhere.

———

I am enough of an artist to draw freely upon my imagination.[3]

———

If you want your children to be intelligent, read them fairy tales. If you want them to be more intelligent, read them more fairy tales.

———

Imagination is everything. It is the preview of life's coming attractions.

———

[1] Quoted by William Miller in *Life Magazine*, May 2, 1955.
[2] From "Was Europe a Success?" (1934), reprinted in *Einstein: Essays in Humanism*, 49.
[3] Quoted in interview by G. S. Viereck, October 26, 1929, reprinted in "Glimpses of the Great" (1930).

When I examine myself and my methods of thought, I come to the conclusion that the gift of fantasy has meant more to me than any talent for abstract, positive thinking.

———

The true sign of intelligence is not knowledge but imagination.

———

Imagination is more important than knowledge. For knowledge is limited to all we now know and understand, while imagination embraces the entire world, and all there ever will be to know and understand.[4]

———

A society's competitive advantage will come not from how well its schools teach the multiplication and periodic tables, but from how well they stimulate imagination and creativity.

———

I have no special talents. I am only passionately curious.

———

Learn from yesterday, live for today, hope for tomorrow.

———

I am not a genius, I am just curious. I ask many questions and when the answer is simple, then God is answering.

———

Creativity is knowing how to hide your sources.

———

Creativity is intelligence having fun.

———

The only sure way to avoid making mistakes is to have no new ideas.

———

Common sense is what tells us the earth is flat.

———

At least once a day, allow yourself the freedom to think and dream

———

[4] "What Life Means to Einstein: An Interview by George Sylvester Viereck," *Saturday Evening Post*, October 26, 1929, p. 17.

for yourself.

––––

I didn't arrive at my understanding of the fundamental laws of the universe through my rational mind.

––––

4

ON LOVE & RELATIONSHIPS

Gravitation is not responsible for people falling in love.[1]

———

Where there is love, there is no imposition.[2]

———

An hour sitting with a pretty girl on a park bench passes like a minute, but a minute sitting on a hot stove seems like an hour.[3]

———

Only a life lived for others is a life worthwhile.[4]

———

Marriage is but slavery made to appear civilized.[5]

[1] To Fred Wall, 1933. *Albert Einstein Archive* 31–845.
[2] Quoted in Sayen, *Einstein in America*, 294.
[3] Quoted by Helen Dukas in Sayen, *Einstein in America*, 130.
[4] Quoted in the *New York Times*, June 20, 1932 *Albert Einstein Archives* 29–041.
[5] Quoted by K. Wachsmann in M. Grüning, *Ein Haus für Albert Einstein*, 159.

Love brings much happiness, much more so than pining for someone brings pain.

Any man who can drive safely while kissing a pretty girl is simply not giving the kiss the attention it deserves.

When you trip over love, it is easy to get up. But when you fall in love, it is impossible to stand again.

The solitude and peace of mind are serving me quite well, not the least of which is due to the excellent and truly enjoyable relationship with my cousin; its stability will be guaranteed by the avoidance of marriage.[6]

[6] To M. Besso, February 12, 1915, *The Collected Papers of Albert Einstein*, Vol. 8, Doc 56.

———

Love is a better master than duty.

———

How on earth can you explain in terms of chemistry and physics so important a biological phenomenon as first love?

———

I have come to know the mutability of all human relationships and have learned to insulate myself against both heat and cold so that a temperature balance is fairly well assured.[7]

———

That little word "WE" I mistrust and here's why:
No man of another can say "He is I".
Behind all agreement lies something amiss
All seeming accord cloaks a lurking abyss.[8]

———

[M]ost men (and also not only a few women) are by nature not monogamous. This nature makes itself even more forceful when tradition and circumstance stand in an individual's way.[9]

———

Men marry women with the hope they will never change. Women marry men with the hope they will change. Invariably they are both disappointed.

———

From the standpoint of daily life, however, there is one thing we do know: that we are here for the sake of each other – above all for those upon whose smile and well-being our own happiness depends, and also for the countless unknown souls with whose fate we are connected by a bond of sympathy. Many times a day I realize how much my own outer and inner life is built upon the labors of my fellow men, both living and dead, and how earnestly I must exert myself in order to give in return as much as I have received.

---

[7] To Heinrich Zangger, March 10, 1917. *Albert Einstein Archives* 39–680.
[8] Quoted in Dukas and Hoffmann, *Albert Einstein: The Human Side*, (1979) 100.
[9] To Dr. Eugenie Anderman, June 2, 1953. *Albert Einstein Archives* 59–097.

———

The best way to cheer yourself is to cheer somebody else up.

———

5

ON FREEDOM

Everything that is really great and inspiring is created by the individual who can labor in freedom.[1]

———

O, Youth: Do you know that yours is not the first generation to yearn for a life full of beauty and freedom?[2]

———

What really interests me is whether God could have created the world any differently; in other words, whether the demand for logical simplicity leaves any freedom at all.[3]

———

The true value of a human being is determined primarily by the measure and the sense in which he has attained liberation from the self.[4]

---

[1] From an address at the commencement exercises of Swarthmore College, 1938.

[2] To I. Stern, 1932, reprinted in Dukas and Hoffmann ed., *Albert Einstein: The Human Side*, (1979) 30. *Albert Einstein Archives* 51–870.

[3] Quoted by Ernst Straus in Seelig, *Helle Zeit, dunkle Zeit*, 72.

[4] From Mein Weltbild (1934). Reprinted in *Ideas and Opinions*, 12.

———

Freedom of teaching and of opinion in book or press is the foundation for the sound and natural development of any people.[5]

———

Politics is a pendulum whose swings between anarchy and tyranny are fueled by perennially rejuvenated illusions.[6]

———

The strength of the Constitution lies entirely in the determination of each citizen to defend it. Only if every single citizen feels duty bound to do his share in this defense are the constitutional rights secure.

———

---

[5] From "At a gathering for freedom of opinion" (1936), reprinted in *Einstein: Essays in Humanism*, 50.
[6] Aphorism, *Albert Einstein Archives* 28–388.

6

ON HUMANITY & STUPIDITY

Two things are infinite: the universe and human stupidity; and I'm
not sure about the universe.

———

The difference between genius and stupidity is; genius has its limits.

———

Everybody is a genius. But if you judge a fish by its ability to climb a
tree, it will live its whole life believing that it is stupid.

———

If a cluttered desk is a sign of a cluttered mind, of what, then, is an
empty desk a sign?

———

It is abhorrent to me when a fine intelligence is paired with an
unsavory character.[1]

———

Any fool can know. The point is to understand.

———

A question that sometimes drives me hazy: am I or are the others
crazy?

---

[1] To Jacob Laub, May 19, 1909. *Albert Einstein Archives* 15–480.

———

Three great forces rule the world: stupidity, fear, and greed.

———

I fear the day technology will surpass our human interaction. The world will have a generation of idiots.

———

With fame I become more and more stupid, which of course is a very common phenomenon.[2]

———

Fear or stupidity has always been the basis of most human actions.[3]

———

I love Humanity, but I hate humans.

———

Somebody who only reads newspapers and at best books of contemporary authors looks to me like an extremely near-sighted person who scorns eyeglasses. He is completely dependent on the prejudices and fashions of his times, since he never gets to see or hear anything else.

———

Without "ethical culture," there is no salvation for humanity.[4]

———

Few people are capable of expressing with equanimity opinions which differ from the prejudices of their social environment. Most people are incapable of forming such opinions.

———

It would be my greatest sadness to see Zionists do to Palestinian Arabs much of what Nazis did to Jews.

———

The human spirit must prevail over technology.

---

[2] To Heinrich Zangger, December 24, 1919. *Albert Einstein Archives* 39–726.

[3] To E. Mulder, April 1954. *Albert Einstein Archives* 60–609.

[4] From "The Need for Ethical Culture," January 5, 1951. *Albert Einstein Archives* 28–904.

———

To obtain an assured favorable response from people, it is better to offer them something for their stomachs instead of their brains.[5]

———

I am thankful to all those who said no. It's because of them, I did it myself.

———

If most of us are ashamed of shabby clothes and shoddy furniture let us be more ashamed of shabby ideas and shoddy philosophies.... It would be a sad situation if the wrapper were better than the meat wrapped inside it.

———

Man is, at one and the same time, a solitary and a social being....[6]

———

The release of atomic power has changed everything except our way of thinking ... the solution to this problem lies in the heart of mankind. If only I had known, I should have become a watchmaker.

———

The man with the greatest soul will always face the greatest war with the low-minded person.

———

A clever person solves a problem. A wise person avoids it.

———

A human being is a part of the whole called by us the universe, a part limited in time and space. He experiences himself, his thoughts and feeling as something separated from the rest, a kind of optical delusion of his consciousness. This delusion is a kind of prison for us, restricting us to our personal desires and to affection for a few persons nearest to us. Our task must be to free ourselves from this prison by widening our circle of compassion to embrace all living creatures and the whole of nature in its beauty.

---

[5] To L. Manners, March 19, 1954. *Albert Einstein Archives* 60–401.
[6] From "Why Socialism?" (1949), reprinted in *Ideas and Opinions*, 153.

———

Great spirits have always encountered violent opposition from mediocre minds.

———

We dance for laughter, we dance for tears, we dance for madness, we dance for fears, we dance for hopes, we dance for screams, we are the dancers, we create the dreams.

———

The intuitive mind is a sacred gift and the rational mind is a faithful servant. We have created a society that honors the servant and has forgotten the gift.

———

It is easier to denature plutonium than to denature the evil spirit of man.[7]

———

The woman who follows the crowd will usually go no further than the crowd. The woman who walks alone is likely to find herself in places no one has ever been before.

———

Force always attracts men of low morality.

———

A foolish faith in authority is the worst enemy of truth.

———

The pursuit of truth and beauty is a sphere of activity in which we are permitted to remain children all our lives.

———

It is harder to crack prejudice than an atom.

———

How I wish that somewhere there existed an island for those who are wise and of good will.

————————

[7] From an interview June 23, 1946, reprinted in *Einstein on Peace*, 385.

———

Small is the number of people who see with their eyes and think with their minds.

———

One of the strongest motives that lead men to art and science is escape from everyday life with its painful crudity and hopeless dreariness, from the fetters of one's own ever-shifting desires. A finely tempered nature longs to escape from the personal life into the world of objective perception and thought.

———

The world will not be destroyed by those who do evil, but by those who watch them without doing anything.

———

7

ON EDUCATION

One had to cram all this stuff into one's mind for the examinations, whether one liked it or not. This coercion had such a deterring effect on me that, after I had passed the final examination, I found the consideration of any scientific problems distasteful to me for an entire year.

———

To me the worst thing seems to be a school principally to work with methods of fear, force and artificial authority. Such treatment destroys the sound sentiments, the sincerity and the self-confidence of pupils and produces a subservient subject.

———

The point is to develop the childlike inclination for play and the childlike desire for recognition and to guide the child over to important fields for society. Such a school demands from the teacher that he be a kind of artist in his province.

———

It is the supreme art of the teacher to awaken joy in creative expression and knowledge.

Teaching should be such that what is offered is perceived as a valuable gift and not as a hard duty.[1]

I never teach my pupils, I only attempt to provide the conditions in which they can learn.

The value of an education in a liberal arts college is not the learning of many facts, but the training of the mind to think something that cannot be learned from textbooks.[2]

---

[1] From "Education for Independent Thought" (1952), reprinted in *Ideas and Opinions*, 67. *Albert Einstein Archives* 60–723.

[2] Quoted in Philipp Frank, *Einstein: His Life and Times*, 185 (1945).

———

Wisdom is not a product of schooling but of the lifelong attempt to acquire it.[3]

———

One should guard against preaching to young people success in the customary form as the main aim in life. The most important motive for work in school and in life is pleasure in work, pleasure in its result, and the knowledge of the value of the result to the community.

———

Truly novel ideas emerge only in one's youth. Later on one becomes more experienced, famous—and foolish.[4]

———

Never regard study as a duty, but as the enviable opportunity to learn to know the liberating influence of beauty in the realm of the spirit for your own personal joy and to the profit of the community to which your later work belongs.

———

The aim [of education] must be the training of independently acting and thinking individuals who, however, see in the service to the community their highest life problem.

———

Only in mathematics and physics was I, through self-study, far beyond the school curriculum, and also with regard to philosophy as it was taught in the school curriculum.[5]

———

Bear in mind that the wonderful things you learn in your schools are the work of many generations. All this is put in your hands as your inheritance in order that you may receive it, honor it, add to it, and one day faithfully hand it on to your children.

---

[3] To J. Dispentiere, March 24, 1954. *Albert Einstein Archives* 59–495.
[4] To Heinrich Zangger, December 6, 1917. *Albert Einstein Archives* 39–689.
[5] Quoted in Hoffmann, *Albert Einstein: Creator and Rebel*, 20.

8

ON WAR

This topic brings me to that worst outcrop of herd life, the military system, which I abhor.... This plague-spot of civilization ought to be abolished with all possible speed. Heroism on command, senseless violence, and all the loathsome nonsense that goes by the name of patriotism – how passionately I hate them!

———

One does not make wars less likely by formulating rules of warfare... War cannot be humanized. It can only be eliminated...

———

An empty stomach is not a good political advisor.

———

Nationalism is an infantile sickness. It is the measles of the human race.[1]

———

We shall require a substantially new manner of thinking if mankind is to survive.

———

[1] Albert Einstein, "The World As I See It" (1934).

The release of atomic energy has not created a new problem. It has merely made more urgent the necessity of solving an existing one.[2]

Why does this applied science, which saves work and makes life easier, bring us so little happiness? The simple answer runs: Because we have not yet learned to make sensible use of it.

We must…dedicate our lives to drying up the source of war: ammunition factories.[3]

---

[2] From "Atomic War or Peace," *Atlantic Monthly*, November 1945.

[3] Published in *Pictorial Review*, February 1933. Quoted in Ronald W. Clark, *Einstein: The Life and Times* (1971).

———

The discovery of nuclear chain reactions need not bring about the destruction of mankind any more than did the discovery of matches. We only must do everything in our power to safeguard against its abuse. Only a supranational organization, equipped with a sufficiently strong executive power, can protect us.

———

Any intelligent fool can make things bigger, more complex, and more violent. It takes a touch of genius – and a lot of courage – to move in the opposite direction.

———

But could not our situation be compared to one of a menacing epidemic? People are unable to view this situation in its true light, for their eyes are blinded by passion. General fear and anxiety create hatred and aggressiveness. The adaptation to warlike aims and activities has corrupted the mentality of man; as a result, intelligent, objective and humane thinking has hardly any effect and is even suspected and persecuted as unpatriotic.[4]

———

He who joyfully marches to music in rank and file has already earned my contempt. He has been given a large brain by mistake, since for him the spinal cord would fully suffice. I would rather be torn to shreds than be a part of so base an action! It is my conviction that killing under the cloak of war is nothing but an act of murder.

———

A Prayer for Understanding: Oh, great Father, never let me judge another man until I have walked in his moccasins for two weeks.

———

Peace cannot be achieved through violence, it can only be attained through understanding.

———

---

[4] Einstein, "The Menace of Mass Destruction" (1947).

Every thoughtful, well-meaning and conscientious human being
should assume in time of peace,
the solemn and unconditional obligation
not to participate in any war, for any reason
or to lend support of any kind, whether direct or indirect.

———

The unleashed power of the atom has changed everything save our
modes of thinking, and thus we drift toward unparalleled catastrophe.

———

The more a country makes military weapons, the more insecure it
becomes: if you have weapons, you become a target for attack.[5]

———

Since I do not foresee that atomic energy is to be a great boon for a
long time, I have to say that for the present it is a menace. Perhaps it
is well that it should be. It may intimidate the human race into
bringing order into its international affairs, which without the
pressure of fear, it would not do.

———

In our time the military mentality is still more dangerous than
formerly because the offensive weapons have become much more
powerful than the defensive ones. Therefore, it leads, by necessity, to
preventive war. The general insecurity that goes hand in hand with
this results in the sacrifice of the citizen's civil rights to the supposed
welfare of the state. Political witch-hunting, controls of all sorts (e.g.,
control of teaching and research, of the press, and so forth) appear
inevitable, and for this reason do not encounter that popular
resistance, which, were it not for the military mentality, would
provide protection. A reappraisal of all values gradually takes place
insofar as everything that does not clearly serve the utopian ends is
regarded and treated as inferior.[6]

———

---

[5] Quoted in interview with A. Aram, January 3, 1953. *Albert Einstein Archives*
59–109.

[6] Albert Einstein, "The Military Mentality."

As long as armies exist, any serious conflict will lead to war. It is characteristic of the military mentality that non-human factors are held essential, while the human being, his desires and thoughts, are considered as unimportant and secondary. You cannot simultaneously prevent and prepare for war. To concentrate on the problems and aspirations which all thinking men share creates a sense of comradeship that is eventually bound to reunite scholars and artists of all nations.

———

He who cherishes the values of culture cannot fail to be a pacifist.[7]

———

The pioneers of a warless world are the youth who refuse military service.

———

A large part of history is replete with the struggle for human rights, an eternal struggle in which final victory can never be won. But to tire in that struggle would mean the ruin of society. Only understanding for our neighbors, justice in our dealings, and willingness to help our fellow men can give human society permanence and assure security for the individual.

———

We scientists, whose tragic destination has been to help in making the methods of annihilation more gruesome and more effective, must consider it our solemn and transcendent duty to do all in our power in preventing these weapons from being used for the brutal purpose for which they were invented. What task could possibly be more important to us? What social aim could be closer to our hearts?

———

Human beings, vegetables, or cosmic dust; we all dance to a mysterious tune, intoned in the distance by an invisible piper.[8]

———

---

[7] Quoted in *Die Friedensbewegung*, Kurt Lenz and Walter Fabian eds. (1922) 17.
[8] Einstein, in *The Saturday Evening Post*, 26 October 1929.

The significant problems we face cannot be solved at the same level of thinking we were at when we created them.

———

I am not only a pacifist, but a militant pacifist. I am willing to fight for peace.... Is it not better for a man to die for a cause in which he believes, such as peace, than to suffer for a cause in which he does not believe, such as war?

———

Few are those who see with their own eyes and feel with their own hearts.

———

In essence, the conflict that exists today is no more than an old-style struggle for power, once again presented to mankind in semi-religious trappings. The difference is that, this time, the development of atomic power has imbued the struggle with a ghostly character; for both parties know and admit that, should the quarrel deteriorate into actual war, mankind is doomed. Despite this knowledge, statesmen in responsible positions on both sides continue to employ the well-known technique of seeking to intimidate and demoralize the opponent by marshaling superior military strength. They do so even though such a policy entails the risk of war and doom. Not one statesman in a position of responsibility has dared to pursue the only course that holds out any promise of peace, the course of supranational security, since for a statesman to follow such a course would be tantamount to political suicide. Political passions, once they have been fanned into flame, exact their victims ... Citater fra...[9]

———

---

[9] EDITOR'S NOTE: Before Einstein died, he left a piece of writing ending in this unfinished sentence.

·9

ON AGING & DEATH

People like you and I, though mortal of course, like everyone else, do not grow old no matter how long we live. What I mean is that we never cease to stand like curious children before the great Mystery into which we were born.[1]

———

I am content in my later years. I have kept my good humor and take neither myself nor the next person seriously.[2]

———

As an elderly man, I have remained estranged from the society here.[3]

———

To one bent on age, death will come as a release. I feel this quite strongly now that I have grown old myself and have come to regard death like an old debt, at long last to be discharged....[4]

[1] To Otto Juliusburger, September 29, 1942.

[2] To P. Moos, March 30, 1950. *Albert Einstein Archives* 60–587.

[3] To Queen Elisabeth of the Belgians, February 16, 1935. *Albert Einstein Archives* 32–385.

[4] To Gertrude Warschauer, February 5, 1955. *Albert Einstein Archives* 39–532.

Strange is our situation here on earth. Each of us comes for a short visit, not knowing why, yet sometimes seeming to divine a purpose.[5]

I wouldn't want to live if I did not have my work.... In any case, it's good that I'm already old and personally don't have to count on a prolonged future.[6]

[5] From "My Credo," 1932. *Albert Einstein Archives* 28–218.
[6] To M. Besso, October 10, 1938. *Albert Einstein Archives* 7–376.

———

My mother has died.... We are all completely exhausted. One feels in one's bones the significance of blood ties.[7]

———

I have remained a simple fellow who asks nothing of the world; only my youth is gone—the enchanting youth that forever walks on air.[8]

———

I have to apologize to you that I am still among the living. There will be a remedy for this, however.[9]

———

I know what it's like to see one's mother go through the agony of death and be unable to help; there is no consolation. We all have to bear such heavy burdens, for they are unalterably linked to life.[10]

———

I myself should also be dead already, but I am still here.[11]

———

[7] To Heinrich Zangger, March 1920, *Albert Einstein Archives* 39–732.
[8] To Anna Meyer-Schmid, May 12, 1909. *Albert Einstein Archives* 44–445.
[9] To Tyfanny Williams, August 25, 1946. *Albert Einstein Archives* 42–612.
[10] To Hedwig Born, June 18, 1920. *Albert Einstein Archives* 8–257.
[11] To E. Schaerer-Meyer, July 27, 1951. *Albert Einstein Archives* 60–525.

10

ON GOD & RELIGION

God does not play dice with the universe.

———

The religion of the future will be cosmic religion. It will transcend personal God and avoid dogma and theology.

———

My religion consists of a humble admiration of the illimitable superior spirit who reveals himself in the slight details we are able to perceive with our frail and feeble mind.

———

If there is any religion that could respond to the needs of modern science, it would be Buddhism.

———

There is nothing divine about [the scientist's] morality; it is a purely human affair.[1]

———

[1] From *Mein Weltbild* (1934), reprinted in *Ideas and Opinions*, 40.

———

No idea is conceived in our mind independent of our five senses [i.e., no idea is divinely inspired].[2]

———

Relativity is a purely scientific matter and has nothing to do with religion.[3]

———

I'm not an atheist and I don't think I can call myself a pantheist. We see a universe marvelously arranged and obeying certain laws, but only dimly understand these laws. Our limited minds cannot grasp the mysterious force that moves the constellations.

———

The bigotry of the nonbeliever is for me nearly as funny as the bigotry of the believer.

———

What I see in Nature is a magnificent structure that we can comprehend only very imperfectly, and that must fill a thinking person with a feeling of humility. This is a genuinely religious feeling that has nothing to do with mysticism.

———

[2] Quoted in W. Hermanns, "A Talk with Einstein." *Albert Einstein Archives* 55–285.

[3] Quoted in Philipp Frank, *Einstein: His Life and Times*, 190.

———

I am also convinced that one gains the purest joy from spiritual things only when they are not tied in with earning one's livelihood.[4]

———

The further the spiritual evolution of mankind advances, the more certain it seems to me that the path to genuine religiosity does not lie through the fear of life, and the fear of death, and blind faith, but through striving after rational knowledge.

———

I do not believe in the immortality of the individual, and I consider ethics to be an exclusively human concern without any superhuman authority behind it.

———

Morality is the highest importance—but for us, not for God.[5]

———

It was, of course, a lie what you read about my religious convictions, a lie which is being systematically repeated. I do not believe in a personal God and I have never denied this but have expressed it clearly. If something is in me which can be called religious then it is the unbounded admiration for the structure of the world so far as our science can reveal it.

———

To sense that behind anything that can be experienced there is a something that our mind cannot grasp and whose beauty and sublimity reaches us only indirectly and as a feeble reflection, this is religiousness. In this sense I am religious.

———

One becomes a deeply religious nonbeliever.... This is a somewhat new kind of religion.[6]

---

[4] To L. Manners, March 19, 1954. *Albert Einstein Archives* 60–401.
[5] To M.M. Schayer, August 1927. *Albert Einstein Archives* 48–380.
[6] To Hans Muehsam, March 30, 1954. *Albert Einstein Archives* 38–434.

———

A forced faithfulness is a bitter fruit for all concerned.[7]

———

God gave me the stubbornness of a mule and a fairly keen scent.[8]

———

Coincidence is God's way of remaining anonymous.

———

God did not create evil. Just as darkness is the absence of light, evil is the absence of God.

———

I cannot imagine a God who rewards and punishes the objects of his creation, whose purposes are modeled after our own – a God, in short, who is but a reflection of human frailty. Neither can I believe that the individual survives the death of his body, although feeble souls harbor such thoughts through fear or ridiculous egotisms.

———

[7] To Dr. Eugenie Anderman, June 2, 1953. *Albert Einstein Archives* 59–097.
[8] Quoted in G.J. Whitrow, "Einstein: the man and his achievement," 91.

———

Black holes are where God divided by zero.

———

I want to know God's thoughts – the rest are mere details.[9]

———

When the solution is simple, God is answering.

———

God is subtle but he is not malicious.

———

The word *God* is for me nothing more than the expression and product of human weaknesses, and religious scripture a collection of honorable, but still primitive legends which are nevertheless pretty childish. No interpretation, no matter how subtle, can (for me) change this.

———

Mysticism is in fact the only criticism people cannot level against my theory.[10]

———

It seems to me that the idea of a personal God is an anthropological concept which I cannot take seriously. I also cannot imagine some will or goal outside the human sphere... Science has been charged with undermining morality, but the charge is unjust. A man's ethical behavior should be based effectually on sympathy, education, and social ties and needs; no religious basis is necessary. Man would indeed be in a poor way if he had to be restrained by fear of punishment and hope of reward after death.

———

What really interests me is whether God had any choice in the creation of the World.

---

[9] Quoted by E. Salaman in "A Talk with Einstein," *Listener* 54 (1955).
[10] Quoted by Ronald W. Clark in *Einstein: The Life and Times*, 268 (1971).

———

The idea of a personal God is quite alien to me and seems even naïve.[11]

———

I don't try to imagine a personal God; it suffices to stand in awe at the structure of the world, insofar as it allows our inadequate senses to appreciate it.

———

Mere unbelief in a personal God is no philosophy at all.[12]

———

I believe in Spinoza's God, who reveals Himself in the lawful harmony of the world, not in a God who concerns Himself with the fate and the doings of mankind...

———

I am a Jew, but I am enthralled by the luminous figure of the Nazarene....No one can read the Gospels without feeling the actual presence of Jesus.

———

[11] To Beatrice Frohlich, December 17, 1952. *Albert Einstein Archives* 59–797.
[12] To V.T. Aaltonen, May 7, 1952. *Albert Einstein Archives* 59–059.

ABOUT THE EDITOR

J. MANHIRE is an attorney and government bureaucrat. He attended Yale, NYU, Regent, Saint Leo, and Villanova, studying mathematics, education, music theory, political philosophy, religious studies, and tax law. He is the author of various journal articles and musical compositions. He lives in Virginia with his wife and nine children, enjoys weight lifting, scotch and cigars with good friends, the intersection of theology and cosmology, anything nautical, and singing *really* loudly to classic rock on the car radio.